First Time

Going to the Library

Melinda Radabaugh

Heinemann Library
Chicago, Illinois

Designed by Sue Emerson, Heinemann Library
Printed and bound in the United States by Lake Book Manufacturing, Inc.

07 06 05 04 03
10 9 8 7 6 5 4 3 2

Library of Congress Cataloging-in-Publication Data
Radabaugh, Melinda Beth.
   Going to the library / Melinda Beth Radabaugh.
      p. cm. -- (First time)
Contents: What is a library? -- Where can you find a library? -- What do libraries look like? -- What can you do at the library? -- What special things does a library have? -- What kinds of books does a library have? -- Who works at a library? -- What is story hour? -- What can you take home with you?
   ISBN 1-4034-0230-2 (HC), 1-4034-0469-0 (Pbk.), 1-4034-3816-1 (BB)
   1. Libraries--Juvenile literature. [1.Libraries .] I. Title. II. Series.
Z665.5 .R34 2002
027--dc21
                                   2002001157

3 3021 00822 7305

Acknowledgments
The author and publishers are grateful to the following for permission to reproduce copyright material:
p. 4 Robin L. Sachs/PhotoEdit, Inc.; p. 5 Mug Shots/Corbisstockmarket.com; p. 6L Michael Paras/International Stock; p. 6R Ken Martin/Visuals Unlimited; p. 7T Guy Cali/Stock Connection/PictureQuest; pp. 7B, 10, 11, 13 Brian Warling/Heinemann Library; p. 12 Jose L. Pelaez/Corbis; pp. 14, 16 Michael Newman/PhotoEdit, Inc.; p. 15 Keith Brofsky/Getty Images; p. 17L Norbert Schiller/Liaison/Getty Images; p. 17R Ed Young/Corbis; p. 18 Robert E. Demmrich/Stone/Getty Images; p. 19 George Ancona/International Stock; p. 20 SW Productions/PhotoDisc; p. 21 Eric Anderson/Visuals Unlimited; p. 22 (row 1, L–R) Heinemann Library, RDF/Visuals Unlimited; p. 22 (row 2, L–R) Heinemann Library, John A. Rizzo/PhotoDisc; p. 22 (row 3, L–R) PhotoDisc, Heinemann Library; p. 23 (row 1, L–R) Heinemann Library, Brian Warling/Heinemann Library, Norbert Schiller/Liaison/Getty Images; p. 23 (row 2, L–R) Ed Young/Corbis, Heinemann Library, Ed Young/Corbis; p. 23 (row 3, L–R) Ed Young/Corbis, Heinemann Library, Heinemann Library; p. 23 (row 4) Heinemann Library; p. 24 Heinemann Library; back cover (L–R) Brian Warling/Heinemann Library, Heinemann Library

Cover photograph by Robin L. Sachs/PhotoEdit, Inc.
Photo research by Amor Montes de Oca

Every effort has been made to contact copyright holders of any material reproduced in this book. Any omissions will be rectified in subsequent printings if notice is given to the publisher.

Special thanks to our advisory panel for their help in the preparation of this book:
Eileen Day, Preschool Teacher
Chicago, IL

Ellen Dolmetsch,
Library Media Specialist
Wilmington, DE

Kathleen Gilbert,
Second Grade Teacher
Round Rock, TX

Sandra Gilbert,
Library Media Specialist
Houston, TX

Angela Leeper,
Educational Consultant
North Carolina Department
of Public Instruction
Raleigh, NC

Pam McDonald,
Reading Support Specialist
Winter Springs, FL

Melinda Murphy,
Library Media Specialist
Houston, TX

We would also like to thank the teachers, staff, and students at Stockton Elementary School in Chicago, Illinois, for their help with this book.

Some words are shown in bold, **like this.**
You can find them in the picture glossary on page 23.

Contents

What Is a Library? 4

Where Can You Find a Library? 6

How Big Are Libraries? 8

What Can You Do at the Library? 10

What Special Things Does
    a Library Have? 12

What Kinds of Books Does
    a Library Have? 14

Who Works at a Library? 16

What Is Story Hour? 18

What Can You Take Home with You? . . 20

Quiz 22

Picture Glossary 23

Note to Parents and Teachers 24

Answers to Quiz 24

Index 24

What Is a Library?

A library has books for everyone.

It is a quiet place to read.

A library is a good place to do school work.

Where Can You Find a Library?

There are libraries in the city.

There are libraries in the country.

Schools have libraries.

There are libraries in classrooms, too.

How Big Are Libraries?

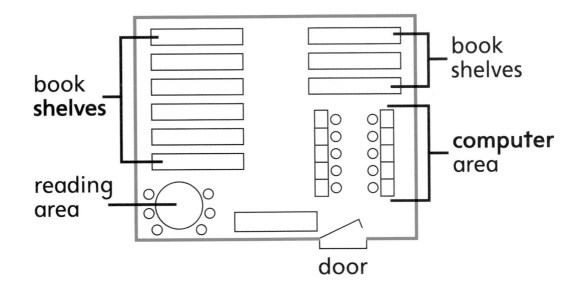

book shelves

book shelves

computer area

reading area

door

Some libraries are very small.

All of the books are in one room.

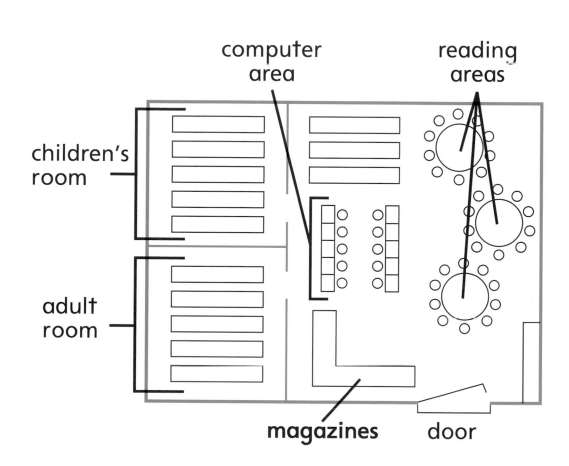

computer area

reading areas

children's room

adult room

magazines   door

Other libraries are big.

The books are in different rooms.

What Can You Do at the Library?

You can look at books.

The books are on **shelves**.

You can read **magazines,** too.

What Special Things Does a Library Have?

Libraries have **computers**.

You can use the computer to find books.

Libraries have **audiotapes.**

You can listen to music or stories.

What Kinds of Books Does a Library Have?

Some books are just for children.

There are **fiction** books and **nonfiction** books.

There are books for grown-ups, too.

There are books about
almost everything!

Who Works at a Library?

Librarians work at the library.

They help people find books to read.

Pages put books on the **shelves.**

Clerks help people check out books.

What Is Story Hour?

Story hour is a special time
for children.

They come to the library to listen
to a story.

The **librarian** reads a book out loud.

Sometimes children help tell a story.

What Can You Take Home with You?

You can take books and **videos** home.

You need a **library card** to check them out.

You can keep the books for a little while.

Don't forget to bring them back to the library!

Quiz

What are some things to do at the library?

Look for the answers on page 24.

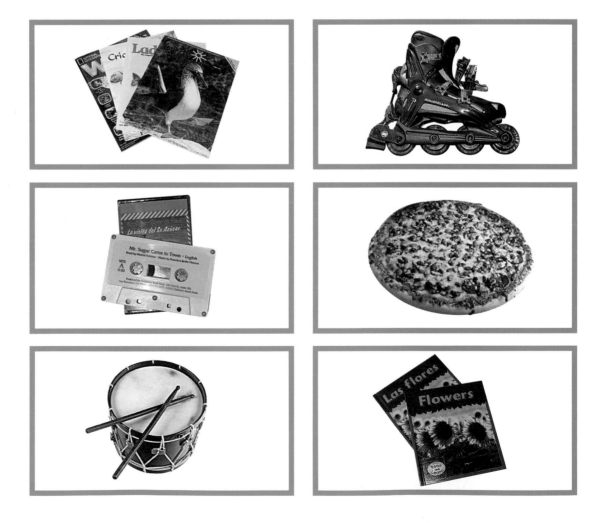

Picture Glossary

audiotape
page 13

librarian
pages 16, 19

page
page 17

clerk
page 17

library card
page 20

shelves
pages 8, 10, 17

computer
pages 8, 9, 12

magazines
pages 9, 11

video
page 20

fiction
page 14

nonfiction
page 14

23

Note to Parents and Teachers

Reading for information is an important part of a child's literacy development. Learning begins with a question about something. Help children think of themselves as investigators and researchers by encouraging their questions about the world around them. Each chapter in this book begins with a question. Read the question together. Look at the pictures. Talk about what you think the answer might be. Then read the text to find out if your predictions were correct. Think of other questions you could ask about the topic, and discuss where you might find the answers. Assist children in using the picture glossary and the index to practice new vocabulary and research skills.

Index

audiotapes 13
books. 4, 8, 9, 10, 12, 14, 15, 16, 17, 19, 20, 21
children 14, 18, 19
clerks 17
computers 8, 9, 12
fiction 14
librarians 16, 19
library card 20
magazines 9, 11
nonfiction 14
pages 17
shelves 8, 10, 17
story hour 18–19
videos 20

Answers to quiz on page 22

read **magazines**

listen to **audiotapes**

read books